CW00435281

Naomi

A Story of a Young Girl With Osteogenesis Imperfecta

by Olivia Shin

Illustrations by MikeMotz.com

This story is dedicated to all the children who have Osteogenesis Imperfecta.

Copyright © 2018 Olivia Shin
No part of this publication may be reproduced,
or stored in a retrieval system, or transmitted by any form
or by any means, electronic, mechanical, photocopying,
recording, or otherwise, without written permission,
except in the context of reviews.

Naomi

A Story
of a Young Girl
With Osteogenesis
Imperfecta

by Olivia Shin

Illustrations by MikeMotz.com

Hello! My name is Naomi. I live with my parents
and the newest member of our family, sweet baby Johnny.

I am almost eight years old and am exactly three feet tall.
I know I am short, but that is because I was born with a
brittle bone disease called Osteogenesis Imperfecta (OI).

Osteogenesis Imperfecta is a condition that makes my bones as fragile as glass. For example, if I accidentally hit my elbow on the kitchen counter, I can easily break those bones.

I was born with a severe type of OI, which makes breaking bones so simple. Out of the eight years I have lived, I have already broken almost 100 bones!

However, I am very lucky to be here today. Many babies born
with OI do not survive, and I was fortunate to be born
with only five fractures. Three of them I broke
while I was in my mother's womb.

When I was born, Mom told me I was crying because breaking bones is extremely painful. Mom did not know what was wrong until the doctor informed her of my rare condition. When she understood all of what the doctor said, Mom was brave enough to step up and raise me in a new lifestyle.

Year by year, the rate I accidentally broke bones lowered
because I learned how to be cautious in every situation.
Sometimes Mom does not let me participate in birthday parties
that are potentially too dangerous to my body. I get upset at first,
but later understand she is just trying to keep me safe.

As a daring girl, I am very limited. There are things that I have
always wanted to try that I will never be able to do,
such as swimming, skiing, and roller skating.

I wish I could give people piggyback rides, bungee jump, and paraglide. Instead, I must constantly be like a shield, protecting this body of mine.

People always feel sorry for me because I break my bones all the time. That is painful for sure, but I don't think it is as painful as trying to fit in with society.

OI does not only make me physically incapable of certain things, but it also makes me look physically different. It can look like I come from a different world, but I am just like any other eight-year-old girl.

My little brother Johnny does not have OI, which I envy.
He will soon be able to do things that I may never be able to do.
Johnny will also look more "normal" than me. Mom does not like
when I say that though.

For example, everybody has a sclerae, which is known
as the white outer layer of our eyeballs.
Mine, however, is a deep blue color.

I am shorter than most people my age. My doctor told me
I wouldn't grow more than three feet, five inches. Although being
short has its downsides, Mommy tells me to always find the bright
side in things. Therefore, I often imagine myself being the same
height as others, but while wearing pretty pink high heels!

Another thing that is different about my appearance
is that I have bowed legs. Therefore, it looks like my legs
go outward from my kneecaps.

This difference causes a lot of people
to stare and whisper about me to others.

It is really hard to fit in with other girls when I look so different from them. Girls are not usually open to hanging out with me because they think that my differences makes me unable to join their group.

One time, a girl told me that she could not be my friend
because I did not look pretty like a princess.

When Mom heard about this, she was furious. She immediately
loaded up our van, buckled me and Johnny into our seats,
and grabbed the car keys. Dad packed my wheelchair in the trunk
and we were off . . . but I wonder where?

I watched out the window as we passed by countless trees, houses, and signs. Then we finally turned a corner and my eyes lit up with wonder. There I saw . . .

. . . a sign which said, "Welcome to the Kingdom of Kindness!"
Dad got out of the car to give our tickets
to the man in the admission booth.

"Hope you have a magical time," he said, and I giggled with excitement.
Dad glanced at me from the rearview mirror and smiled, too.

Once we found parking, Dad unbuckled Johnny and put him
in his stroller. Mom placed me in my wheelchair and kneeled in front
of me. "Now that you are in your carriage, are you ready to meet
your other royal friends, Princess?" Mom asked. I clapped my hands
and squirmed with joy as I nodded.

Mom and Dad booked us a lunch with the princesses at the "Castle of Courtesy." They were all dressed in beautiful gowns of silk. Their hair glimmered in the light from their bejeweled tiaras, and their faces sparkled as they smiled down on me.

"Welcome, Princess Naomi!" one of the princesses said.
"We are so excited to eat a royal lunch with you!"

A man in white led us to our table, and my family and I walked with princesses to our seats.

We talked. We laughed. We smiled. As we enjoyed a delicious meal, one of the princesses told me that I was the ultimate princess because I was so strong at heart. She then crowned me with a tiara of sparkling jewels. It was the most magical moment in the world, and I did not want to ever leave.

On the car ride home, I wondered what my life would like if I didn't have OI. I could be the most popular girl at school! But then I thought about what I learned today and the vision vanished from my head immediately.

My visit to the Kingdom of Kindness taught me something valuable about the definition of beauty. I realized that the princesses I met at the Castle of Courtesy were not known for their external beauty, but for their internal beauty — their compassion and love.

I also learned that if I didn't have OI, I would not be Naomi.
I would be someone else.

People are different. Everyone. And "normal" is also different for everyone. In my opinion, it is just an ambiguous word that can let people down if they think about it too much.

I happen to have more differences than most, but that doesn't mean I should reject myself because of it. What makes me different is what makes me unique, and I should embrace every aspect of myself-Naomi Clark!

Even though I am extremely fragile, I am also strong- strong
because I now know how to embrace the unique beauties
of myself as gifts in my life. Now that is a TRUE princess!

Acknowledgements

GO FROGS!

Chelsea Ban, MD
Specialty: OB/GYN
at Oregon Health and Science
University Medical Director
at Borland Free Clinic
Lake Oswego, OR 97034

TCU
John V. Roach Honors College

This project was partially funded
by the TCU John V. Roach Honors
College to help me continue my
undergraduate research on my
mission to promote awareness of
disabilities to the young children through children's books.

TCU College of Education:
Alice Neeley Special Education
Research & Service Institute
This project was partially funded by the TCU
College of Education Alice Neeley Special Education
Research & Service Institute. Views and opinions
expressed in this publication are those of the author
and do not necessarily reflect the policy or position
of TCU, the COE, or the ANSWERS Institute.

be proud

About the Author

Olivia Shin is 19 years old and currently attends Texas Christian University in Fort Worth, Texas. She is an Early Childhood Education major with an emphasis in Special Education, hoping to one day pursue teaching and inspire young kids. Although she wrote this book at 17 years old, Shin finally got it published two years later with the help of TCU. Naomi is her second book in her children's series, which aims to remove the negative stigma that accompanies children with disabilities and educate young kids about the power of celebrating uniqueness.

Although Osteogenesis is an orphan disease, Shin believes it is just as important to educate children about OI as it is for any other disability because it is something individuals may identify with, and every child matters. Shin says, "We live in a world that is always in need of extra grace, compassion, and empathy, and I want my books to be a step towards that direction."

Printed in Great Britain
by Amazon

29380379R00023